Amazing Animals

SNAKES

Jen Green

FRANKLIN WATTS
LONDON • SYDNEY

An Appleseed Editions book

First published in 2010 by Franklin Watts

Franklin Watts
338 Euston Road, London NW1 3BH

Franklin Watts Australia
Level 17/207 Kent St, Sydney, NSW 2000

© 2010 Appleseed Editions

Appleseed Editions Ltd
Well House, Friars Hill, Guestling, East Sussex TN35 4ET

Created by Q2AMedia
Editor: Katie Dicker
Art Director: Harleen Mehta
Designer: Dibakar Acharjee
Picture Researcher: Sujatha Menon
Line Artist: Parwinder Singh Soni
Colouring Artist: Abhijeet Sharma

ISBN 978 1 4451 0004 3

Dewey classification: 597.9'6

All words in **bold** can be found in the Glossary on pages 30–31.

Website information is correct at the time of going to press. However, the publishers cannot
accept liability for any information or links found on third-party websites.

A CIP catalogue for this book is available from the British Library.

Picture credits
t=top b=bottom c=centre l=left r=right
Cover images: Index Stock Imagery/Photolibrary, Roman Mostakov/Fotolia

Cory Thoemke/Istockphoto: Title page, Fotosav/Shutterstock: Contents page, Carey Alan & Sandy/Photolibrary: 4, James Steidl/
Istockphoto: 5t, Rich & Galina Leighton/Dreamstime: 5b, Lawrence Wee/Dreamstime: 6, Kathie Atkinson/Photolibrary: 7,
Gerald Deboer/Dreamstime: 8, Michael Fogden/Photolibrary: 9, Gunter Ziesler/Photolibrary: 10, Stan Osolinski/Photolibrary: 11,
Zigmund Leszczynski/Photolibrary: 12, Mark Kostich/Istockphoto: 13, Omar Ariff Kamarul Ariffin/Dreamstime: 14,
Anthony Bannister/Photolibrary: 15, Gasparetz Attila/Istockphoto: 16, Joe Mc Donald/Photolibrary: 17, Cory Thoemke/
Istockphoto: 18, Herrmann D/Photolibrary: 19, John Cancalosi/NHPA: 20, Mark Hamblin/Photolibrary: 21t, Norbert Rosing/
National Geographic/Getty Images: 21b, Wayne Lynch/Photolibrary: 22, Zigmund Leszczynski/Photolibrary: 23t,
Daniel Heuclin/NHPA: 23b, Secret Sea Visions/Photolibrary: 24, Paul Freed/Photolibrary: 25t, Tobias Bernhard/
Photolibrary: 25b, Gladskikh Tatiana/Shutterstock: 26bl, Tatyana Gladskikh/Dreamstime: 26br,
Evaletova/Dreamstime: 26bc, Carri Keill/Istockphoto: 27l, Archana Bhartia/Dreamstime: 27r,
Chris Mattison/Photolibrary: 28, Neeraj Mishra/Ecoscene: 29, Mark Kostich/Istockphoto: 31.

Q2AMedia Art Bank: 8, 11, 14.

Printed in China

Franklin Watts is a division of Hachette Children's Books,
an Hachette Livre UK company.
www.hachettelivre.co.uk

Contents

Legless reptiles

Snakes are a truly amazing group of animals. They have no legs, but can move around smoothly and silently. They have no claws, but capture and kill all their food. In fact, snakes are some of the world's deadliest animals. They are expert killers.

Armed and deadly

Many people are frightened of snakes. This is partly because their bodies are so different to ours, and because they move by **slithering**. But the main reason is that some snakes are armed with deadly poison. Snakes such as sea kraits have quick-acting poison that kills their **prey** in seconds. In other **species**, the **venom** acts more slowly, so the victim dies a slow, painful death. Not all snakes are poisonous, however. Only about one-tenth of all snakes have poison strong enough to kill a person.

Snakes can be frightening, especially if you meet one unexpectedly. Some snakes are very dangerous.

The western diamondback rattlesnake is the deadliest snake in North America

Tail is slimmer
than main body

Scaly skin

Slender body is muscular
and flexible (bendy)

Wide head

Forked tongue

Snakes have no eyelids

Snakes have a
slender body
covered with scales.

Reptile family

There are nearly 3,000 different
species of snake, living in most
parts of the world. Like other
reptiles, snakes have a dry, scaly
skin, and many breed by laying
eggs. While most reptiles have four
legs, snakes are legless. Their forked
tongue is also unusual. Apart from
two types of lizard, snakes are the
only reptiles that are poisonous.

All snakes eat meat.
This snake is eating
a frog head-first!

THE DEADLY MAMBA

The black mamba is one of the
world's deadliest snakes. This fast-
moving snake found in African
woodlands grows to 4 metres long.
Its poison is so powerful it can kill
a person in just ten minutes.

Slithering along

Despite their lack of legs, snakes are quite fast and agile. They can slither over the ground, weave through water and shin up trees. Some snakes can even glide through the air!

Snake shapes

Snakes are basically long and slender, but they do have different shapes. Pythons are large with fat bodies. Vipers are short. Vine snakes are long and thin. Different shapes help snakes to get about in their particular **habitat**, whether on land, in water or high in trees. Tree and burrowing snakes are long and slim. Sea snakes have flattish bodies that push against the water. Water snakes called anacondas can get very heavy and still be active, because the water supports their great weight.

Belly scales have little ridges that grip the bark

Tree snakes such as this paradise tree snake are slim and light, which helps them to climb trees.

Getting about

Snakes slither along the ground by flexing their muscular bodies. Most snakes move by throwing their body into S-shaped curves. Their flat belly scales push against the ground. Water snakes swim using a similar technique. Tree snakes use their ridged belly scales to grip the bark. Some snakes move by bunching their body into tight coils and then stretching it out like a **concertina**.

The black mamba is the fastest snake on land. It can slither at up to 19 kph over a short distance – as fast as you can run. Black racer snakes in North America are also very fast, with a top speed of 10 kph.

'FLYING' SNAKES

'Flying' snakes live in the forests of Southeast Asia. They cannot really fly, but glide down from high trees. As the snake launches itself into the air, it spreads its ribs to make its body wider. Its belly curves inwards. This shape acts like a parachute. The snake glides gently down and lands smoothly.

Wide belly scales act like caterpillar tracks on a tank, gripping the ground

A snake curves its body to slither forward. The curves push against the ground to move the snake along.

Crafty hunters

All snakes are **carnivores**. Their prey includes mammals, birds, fish, frogs, insects, reptiles... in fact, almost every type of animal on the planet! Some snakes target one particular food – such as eggs or insects. Other snakes eat just about anything they can sink their teeth into.

Snakes have no outside ears, but they can hear

Eye

Nostril

Forked tongue is used for smelling and tasting

Most of the snake's senses are on its head.

Sharp senses

Like all **predators**, snakes rely on their senses to find food. Their main senses are smell, taste and touch. The snake's flickering tongue collects scents in the air. It touches its tongue against the roof of its mouth to identify these scents. Snakes cannot hear well, but they can sense the ground shaking as animals pass by.

Some snakes can see quite well, but they are only good at spotting things that move. Snakes that hunt at night have special senses that help them to find their prey in the dark.

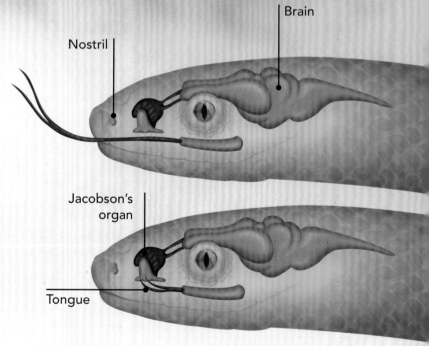

Brain

Nostril

Jacobson's organ

Tongue

The snake identifies scents on its tongue using pits in the roof of its mouth called the Jacobson's organ.

This snake has just swallowed a whole egg.

Bulge is an egg still in its shell

Egg will soon be broken

The snake will eat the contents and spit out the shell

Ways of hunting

Some snakes are active hunters. They slither up to their prey until they are close enough to strike, or drop down from trees. Others lie in wait, and grab passing prey. The snake wraps its body around its victim so it can't escape.

Snakes called **constrictors** kill their prey by squeezing very tightly. A snake's main weapons are its teeth. Snakes such as cobras and vipers have special long, sharp teeth called **fangs**, which they use to inject their prey with poison. Snakes swallow their prey whole – dead or alive.

LURING PREY

Cottonmouths lurk in swamps in the southeastern USA. This mainly brown snake has a thin, yellow tail-tip, which looks like a worm. It wriggles its tail to attract prey such as birds. As the bird moves close to grab the 'worm', the snake strikes with lightning speed.

9

Death by squeezing

Pythons and boas squeeze their prey to death. The snake winds its body around its victim and tightens its coils. This is called constriction. Boas and pythons are the largest snakes in the world.

Huge prey

It is dusk on the African grasslands. A large rock python has caught a gazelle by a waterhole. It holds its prey in its enormous jaws and wraps its muscular body around it. Every time the gazelle breathes out, the snake squeezes a little tighter. Soon the gazelle cannot breathe, and dies of **suffocation**.

Boas and pythons are able to swallow prey as large as gazelles thanks to their huge jaws, which can open very wide. The jawbones are loosely connected with stretchy fibre. The jaw works like a double hinge. The lower jaw can even **dislocate** – separate from the rest of the skull. This allows the snake to swallow an animal wider than its own head.

A rock python tightens its coils to suffocate a gazelle.

Coils tighten every time the prey breathes out

Prey is swallowed head-first

Massive meal

Snakes cannot chew their food – instead they swallow it whole. Their stomach juices get to work dissolving the animal's body. Digestion can take a week in the case of a large meal, but this will keep the snake going for a month or more.

This python is 'walking' its jaws over an impala to swallow it whole.

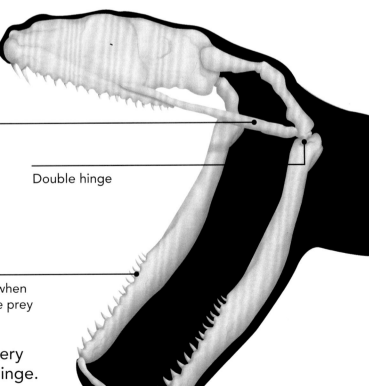

Stretchy fibres called ligaments link the bones of the jaw

Double hinge

Lower jawbone disconnects when the snake swallows very large prey

A snake's jaws can open very wide thanks to a double hinge.

Scaly skin

Scales cover every inch of a snake's body, even its eyes. Scales are thick, tough pieces of skin. They protect the snake from injury and also from the weather. A snake's scales act like a suit of armour, but are light and flexible, so it can move about freely.

Peeling off

Scales are made of a tough, horny material called **keratin**. Your nails and hair are made of the same material. But like a suit of armour, a snake's scaly skin doesn't grow with the rest of its body. When its skin gets too tight, the snake sheds it in one piece. This is called **sloughing** or **moulting**. The dead outer layer peels off to reveal a new, bright, shiny skin.

Adult snakes moult several times a year. Young snakes moult more often as they grow.

Eye is protected by a see-through scale called a brill

Snake rubs itself against a rock to peel off the skin

Skin comes off inside out

Marks of scales show on the moulted skin

Markings break up the
snake's outline

Brown and cream
patches match
fallen leaves

The gaboon viper is
invisible against the
leaves – until it is too late.

Disguise and warning

Most snakes are dull green or brown,
with markings that blend in with their
surroundings. This is called **camouflage**.
It helps the snake to hide from its enemies
and sneak up on its prey.

A few snakes have bright colours that warn
other animals of its deadly poison. Animals
recognise the bright colours and keep away.
Some snakes that are not poisonous copy
the same colours. Harmless milk snakes
look like poisonous coral snakes, with bright
red, black and yellow bands. Their copy-cat
colours fool enemies into avoiding them, too.

PERFECT DISGUISE

The gaboon viper found
in African woodlands is a
camouflage expert. Its black,
brown and cream markings
merge with the leaves and
shadows on the forest floor.
It lurks among the leaves,
keeping perfectly still. When
a victim comes within range,
it strikes with its poison!

The deadly cobra

Cobras are deadly snakes from Africa and Asia. Venom (poison) helps them to quickly kill their prey, so they don't get scratched or bitten. But these snakes prefer to slither away from an enemy. They only use their poison as a last resort if their camouflage fails.

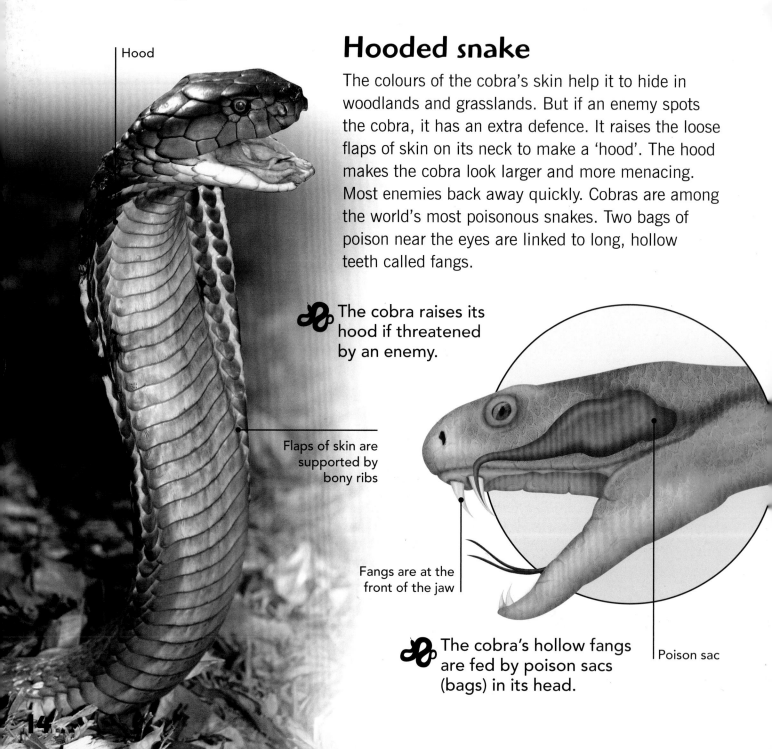

Hood

Hooded snake

The colours of the cobra's skin help it to hide in woodlands and grasslands. But if an enemy spots the cobra, it has an extra defence. It raises the loose flaps of skin on its neck to make a 'hood'. The hood makes the cobra look larger and more menacing. Most enemies back away quickly. Cobras are among the world's most poisonous snakes. Two bags of poison near the eyes are linked to long, hollow teeth called fangs.

The cobra raises its hood if threatened by an enemy.

Flaps of skin are supported by bony ribs

Fangs are at the front of the jaw

Poison sac

The cobra's hollow fangs are fed by poison sacs (bags) in its head.

Injecting poison

As the cobra strikes, its fangs inject a deadly mix of chemicals. This stops the victim's heart and lungs working, and the prey dies within minutes. The venom also starts to digest the prey before the snake has even swallowed it! The king cobra is the world's largest venomous snake, growing up to 5.7 metres long. Its poison is strong enough to kill an elephant!

Spitting venom

Spitting cobras have openings in the front of their hollow fangs. This allows them to spit venom at an attacker. The snake aims for its enemy's eyes. Its poison causes great pain. A person can go blind temporarily if the poison gets into his or her eyes.

The spitting cobra squirts venom at its enemies.

Snake country

Snakes live on every continent except Antarctica. In most parts of the world, you'll find at least one snake that is poisonous. However, snakes aren't found on islands in the middle of vast oceans, because they can't swim great distances.

Cold-blooded creatures

Most snakes live in hot places, such as countries around the **Equator**. This is because, like other reptiles, they are 'cold-blooded'. Their body temperature is always similar to their surroundings. Snakes need warmth from the Sun to be active, so they sunbathe in the early morning. If a snake gets too hot, it moves into the shade. Snakes can't survive in very cold places such as the Arctic or on high, snowy mountains.

Rainforest snakes coil around branches waiting for prey.

Lightweight body helps the snake slither about in trees

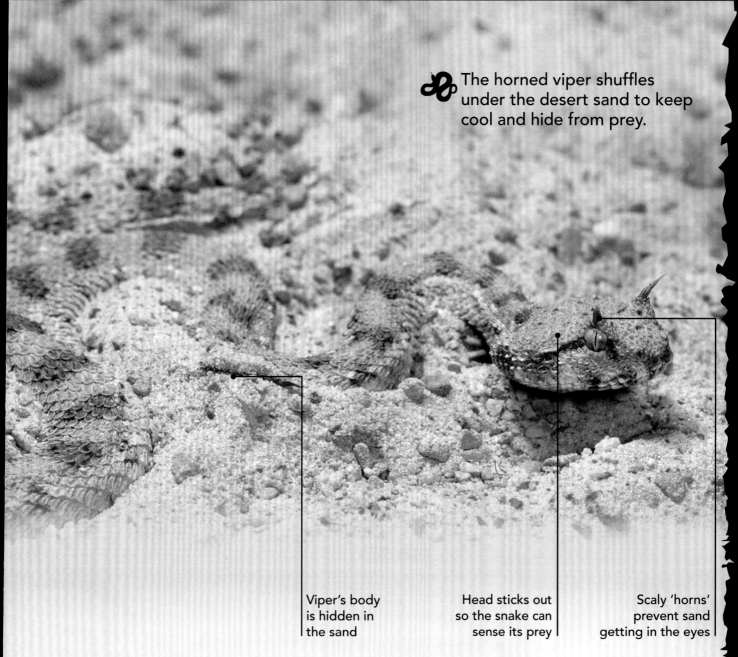

The horned viper shuffles under the desert sand to keep cool and hide from prey.

| Viper's body is hidden in the sand | Head sticks out so the snake can sense its prey | Scaly 'horns' prevent sand getting in the eyes |

Snake homes

Snakes live in all kinds of habitat, including forests, grasslands, heaths and deserts. Some species slither or swim in swamps, rivers and oceans. Snakes are most plentiful in tropical rainforests that are rich in prey such as frogs, birds and insects. Surprisingly, deserts are also good snake territory. Desert snakes survive the heat by hiding in the shade by day, and hunting at night.

AUSTRALIAN TERRORS

Australia has more poisonous snakes than any other country. The world's deadliest snakes include the inland taipan and the Australian tiger snake. Venomous sea snakes swim in Australian coastal waters.

Rattlesnakes

Rattlesnakes are vipers that live in the deserts and scrublands of North America. They are named after the rattling sound they make with their tails. The rattle warns enemies that the snake is armed with fast-acting poison.

Hunting in darkness

Rattlesnakes mostly hunt at night. They track their prey in darkness using special heat-sensing pits on their faces. These little pits pick up the body heat of animals. The snake moves its head to pinpoint its prey in complete darkness. As it strikes, its long fangs swing forward to inject venom. If the prey manages to escape, it soon drops dead in its tracks. The rattlesnake follows the scent trail to its meal.

Many people have died from the poison of a rattlesnake's bite.

The snake cannot hear its own rattle, but enemies can!

Warning rattle

Rattlesnakes shake their tails to warn away enemies, such as cattle, that might tread on them. When a cow hears a loud hiss and scary buzzing sound, it knows to back away quickly. The snake's rattle is made of loose scales. Every time the snake moults, a button of dead skin is left on the tail, to form a new **segment** of the rattle. So the snakes with the longest rattles are usually the oldest and most experienced.

DEADLY RATTLER

The western diamondback is the most dangerous rattlesnake in North America. This rattler is armed with deadly venom, and will hold its ground and strike rather than slither away. It lives in all sorts of habitat in the southwestern USA, including deserts, fields and gardens, where it may lurk in a pile of wood.

Sidewinders

Sidewinders are desert rattlesnakes. These snakes slither sideways, leaving a telltale line of J-shaped tracks. Only a small part of the snake's body touches the hot sand at any time.

Head and tail grip the ground while the body moves sideways

The sidewinder rattlesnake moves sideways. This movement is called sidewinding.

Line of J-shaped tracks

Winter sleep

Snakes that live in cool parts of the world spend the winter sleeping. This is no ordinary sleep, but a very deep sleep called **hibernation**. On the cold, windy plains of Russia, adders spend up to eight months asleep.

Ready to rest

Snakes need to be warm to move about and hunt. In cold weather, they get sluggish – they cannot hunt effectively or escape from danger. A snake could even freeze to death if caught in the open. So when the frosty days of autumn arrive, snakes hide away in caves, hollow logs or abandoned burrows, and prepare to sleep. Some snakes gather in large groups to hibernate. Hibernating in a mass helps the snakes to keep warm.

These timber rattlesnakes have been hibernating in a group to keep warm.

Dead to the world

During hibernation, the snake's body temperature drops to almost freezing point. Its heart and other body processes slow down, so it uses up very little energy. The reptile looks dead, but when warm weather returns in spring, it 'comes alive' again. It crawls out of its hidey-hole and basks in the sunshine to warm its muscles. Having not eaten for many months, the snake is starving hungry. It will strike any prey it comes across.

An adder warms itself after its long winter sleep.

Rocky crevice provides a safe place to sleep

GARTER SNAKES

Garter snakes live the furthest north of any snake in North America. Up to a thousand of these snakes may gather to hibernate in logs and rocky crevices. Like adders, they spend up to eight months asleep.

These red-sided garter snakes are coming out from their winter den.

Baby snakes

Snakes breed in different ways. Many snakes lay eggs that hatch into mini-versions of their parents. In other species, the babies develop inside the mother. As with humans, the female gives birth to living young.

Mating time

In warm countries, snakes breed at any time of year. In cool areas, they usually breed in spring, as soon as they awake from hibernation. This gives the babies a long time to grow before winter returns. Before breeding, male snakes hold wrestling contests to find out who is strongest. Only the champions get the chance to mate.

These male garter snakes are trying to attract a female to breed.

Hatching out

Cobras, pythons and rat snakes lay leathery-shelled eggs a few weeks after mating. Most snakes lay up to 30 eggs, but large pythons lay up to 100! The eggs are laid in a warm, sheltered spot, such as a compost heap. The babies hatch two to four months later.

Tough babies

Female rattlesnakes look after their young for a few weeks, but most baby snakes are alone as soon as they hatch. Don't feel too sorry for them – young snakes can take care of themselves. They are born with the hunting instinct, and go after small prey such as insects and lizards. Baby adders and rattlesnakes are armed with sharp fangs and poison. They can give you a nasty bite.

CARING COBRA

The female king cobra is the only snake to build a nest. She sits on her eggs to protect them from enemies. Her body heat makes the eggs develop faster. After two months on guard without eating, the hungry female leaves the nest just before the babies hatch.

The female king cobra lays her eggs in a nest of leaves and twigs.

Sea snakes

Most people think of snakes as land animals, but many types of snake live in salt or fresh water. Scientists believe that sea snakes probably outnumber land snakes. However, we know very little about these mysterious sea-going creatures.

Suited to the sea

Sea snakes live in warm seas and oceans. Like other reptiles, they need to breathe air. Snakes have one long, slim lung inside their body, but sea snakes have an extra-large lung. They can stay underwater for two hours or more. Nostrils on the top of their snout mean the snake can breathe without lifting its whole head out of the water.

The sea snake's tail is flattened like an oar. It swims by weaving through the water, swishing its tail. Some snakes can swim backwards as well as forwards!

Tail sweeps the water aside

Sea snakes can dive to 150 metres

Long, slim lung holds air

A swimming sea snake uses its tail like an oar.

Hunting in water

Sea snakes prey on ocean creatures such as fish, prawns, squid and crabs. Eels are a favourite prey, because they are just the right shape to fit inside the snake's body! Sea snakes are armed with strong, quick-acting poison, so their victim drops dead before it can escape into the ocean depths. Most snakes hunt in shallow coastal waters, but yellow-bellied sea snakes hunt out in the open ocean.

The yellow-bellied sea snake looks amongst seaweed for fish to eat.

Coloured bands warn that the snake is very poisonous

Snake returns to the beach where it hatched out to breed

A banded sea krait slithers up a beach to lay her eggs.

BREEDING AT SEA

Most sea snakes never come on land. They mate and give birth to living young in the water. But sea kraits come ashore on remote beaches to mate. Later, the females return to lay their eggs in caves beyond the high tide mark.

25

Snakes and people

Snakes have many natural enemies, but people are their greatest threat. Humans kill snakes because they see them as dangerous. They also harm snakes by taking over the wild places where they live. Most snakes are actually harmless to humans, and some are even helpful!

Hunting snakes

For centuries, people have hunted snakes, especially poisonous ones. When the American West was first settled, people used to hold 'rattlesnake round-ups' – organised hunts to clear the land of deadly rattlers. In some parts of the world, snakes are hunted for food. Snakes feature on the menu in Africa, Asia and Australia. People also use snakeskin to make belts, boots and handbags. In China, snakes are used to make traditional medicine.

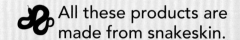 All these products are made from snakeskin.

Disappearing habitats

All over the world, snake habitats are disappearing as people take over wild areas. Forests are cut down, and heaths and swamps are bulldozed to build new roads and towns. This has made some types of snake very rare.

Helpful snakes

Snakes can be helpful as well as harmful. In Asia, some people keep snakes in barns and even houses to kill mice and rats. Snake charmers from India use cobras in shows. In America, poisonous snakes are used in some religious ceremonies. Snakes are part of the natural world. We need to protect them, just as we protect cuddly-looking animals, such as pandas and polar bears.

ANTIVENOM

Antivenom is a medicine used to treat snake bites. It is made using snake poison. Captive snakes are 'milked' for their venom. The snake is made to bite a foam pad or plastic dish. The poison trickles down and is saved to make antivenom.

Some people keep snakes as pets, but these reptiles are much happier in the wild.

27

Facts and records

Snakes are record-breaking reptiles. They include the world's heaviest reptile and are some of the longest and deadliest creatures on Earth.

The blind snake is so tiny it would easily fit inside a straw.

Largest and smallest

- The world's largest snakes are pythons and boas that kill by squeezing.

- The reticulated python of Southeast Asia is the world's longest snake. It measures up to 10 metres long and eats creatures as large as deer.

- The green anaconda is the world's heaviest snake, growing up to 8 metres long and weighing 227 kg – that's the length of a bus and the weight of four adults!

- The world's smallest snakes are blind snakes and thread snakes. They live underground and measure just 10 cm long.

Lucky escape!

In 2009, a farm worker from East Africa survived an epic battle with a 4-metre python. The snake attacked after the man trod on it by accident. It coiled its huge body around him and hauled him into a tree! During a three-hour struggle, the man prevented the snake from swallowing him by wrapping his shirt over its mouth. He was finally rescued by police after calling for help on his mobile phone.

Did you know?

- Snakes hiss when they force air through their narrow throat. The sound is a way of saying 'stay away'!
- Anacondas eat such big meals that they only need to feast four or five times a year.
- The venom from a Brazilian pit viper is used in a drug to treat high blood pressure.
- Some desert snakes, such as African rock pythons, enter a deep sleep to survive the hottest, driest time of year. This summer sleep, similar to hibernation, is called aestivation.

Body facts

- Snakes carry on growing throughout their lives so the biggest snakes are often the oldest.
- A snake is able to push its windpipe forward to the front of its mouth. The windpipe acts as a snorkel while the snake swallows its prey – a process which can take up to an hour.
- The gaboon viper has the longest fangs of any snake, more than 5 cm long.

Names and numbers

- Snakes have at least 100 bones in their back, some species have more than 400. These bones give the snake flexibility and movement.
- Some snakes have more than 200 teeth. The teeth aren't used for chewing, but point backwards to grip prey and prevent it from escaping.
- The word cobra means 'hooded'.

Some cobras have large spots on the back of their hood, that look like eyes. This makes the snake look scary even from behind!

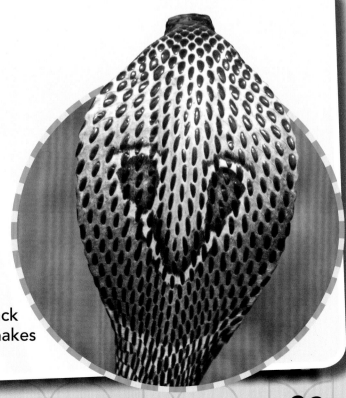

Glossary

antivenom
a medicine used to treat poisonous snake bites

camouflage
the colours and patterns on an animal's skin, fur or feathers that help it blend with its surroundings, so that it is hard to see

carnivore
an animal that eats meat

concertina
a musical instrument that is squeezed and stretched

constrictor
a snake that kills its prey by squeezing it to death

dislocate
when a bone comes out of its socket

equator
the imaginary line around the Earth's middle

fang
a long, pointed tooth that can be used to inject poison

habitat
a particular place where plants and animals live, such as a tropical forest or desert

hibernation
a deep sleep that allows animals to survive the cold of winter

keratin
the tough, horny material of which a snake's scales are made

moult
when an animal sheds its skin

predator
an animal that hunts others for food

prey
an animal that is eaten for food by another

reptile
a group of vertebrates (animals with a backbone) that usually have a scaly skin and lay eggs. Snakes are reptiles

segment
a section of something. The tail of a rattlesnake has different segments

slither
to slip and slide along

sloughing
when a snake sheds its skin in one piece

species
a particular type of animal, such as a king cobra

suffocation
when an animal dies because it cannot breathe

venom
the poison of a snake which is often deadly

Index

Web finder

Kidszone
www.kidzone.ws/lw/snakes/facts.htm
Find out about different types of snake and how they move and hunt.

Kids Konnect
www.kidskonnect.com/content/view/50/27
Full of facts about snakes, from rattlesnakes to thread snakes.

Tigerhomes.org
www.tigerhomes.org/animal/poisonous-snakes.cfm
Learn about the world's most poisonous snakes.

Enchanted Learning
www.enchantedlearning.com/subjects/reptiles/snakes/Boa.shtml
Find out more about the constrictors that suffocate their prey.

Animal Planet
www.animal.discovery.com/fansites/crochunter/australiazoo/10mostvenomous.html
Learn more about Australia's most deadly snakes.